# Flowers

# In

# Winter

THANDIWE MCMILLAN

*Flowers In Winter copyright* © 2021 by Thandiwe McMillan

ISBN: 978-1-7366301-0-5 (ebook)
ISBN: 978-1-7366301-2-9 (Paperback)
ISBN: 978-1-7366301-1-2 (Hardcover)

For more information, please visit:
thandiwemcmillan.com

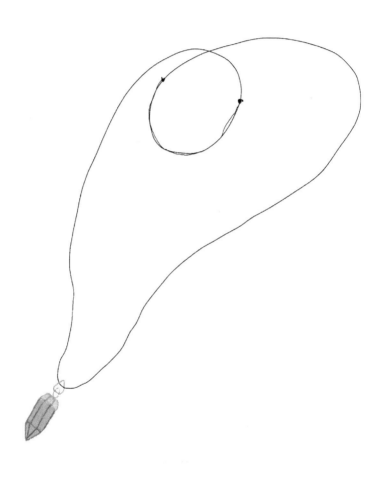

My darling Benjamín, this book is for you. Not a day passes that I don't think of you. I will love you forever.

## Acknowledgements

I would like to thank everyone who purchased this
book during the pre-launch. This publication would
not have been possible without all of you and for
that I am eternally grateful. I often think of all the
experiences in my life that led to me writing this
book. Although some of those memories bring tears
to my eyes, there have also been joyous moments. I
hope that you read this book and find something
that resonates with you whether that be a line, a
stanza, or entire poems. Lastly, I hope that by the
time you finish this book you have more hope in
your heart than when you arrived on this page.

Now, shall we begin?

Flowers in Winter,
half bent and swaying.
Withering beauties refusing
to blow away like sand,
you press on.
Devour slivers of light on
Winter's short days,
and face the fiery star of hope,
though she seldom shows her
face.

# Contents

I pick words, like fruit
from tropical trees, and
pour them on blank pages.

Vivid thoughts displayed.
My life, an exhibition;
and rich poems are born.

# Part I:
## Discovery & Belonging

## THANDIWE MEANS BELOVED

Only four syllables, yet a mouthful.
A bitter, foreign word on my tongue
Community
I spit it out.

Here is where I expected to find place.
Here is where I sank into a sofa
among a sea of black faces who peered at me.
I introduced myself
Thandiwe
A Zulu name meaning beloved.
I don't feel love.

Here is where I expected to find place.
Here is where I had uprooted my spikes
from that other world—
*that world with people who don't look like me—*
to raise my hand in solidarity with my own.
I introduced myself
Thandiwe
and asked, what if I don't have a community?
I am told that I must.

Loneliness knows my name;
it is a Zulu word meaning, beloved.

## YOUTH

Take two long, brown,
thin, cinnamon stick legs.
Mix with slender hands,
clumsy dancing feet,
braised caramelized skin.
Knead her into a lanky,
clumsy thirteen year old.
Dress her in flowery jeans
and graphic tees.
Simmer her in shyness,
with a pinch of attitude.
Sprinkle a dash of curiosity
Glaze her tenderly with
strips of affection.
Sauté her in a pan
of youth
watch her marinate.

## What this voice can do

This is not a small voice.
This voice is crisp,
sharp,
This voice stands alone,
speaks its mind.

It is the voice heard from
the back of auditoriums,
that turns heads
with what it has to say.

This voice holds power.

This voice will
not be muted.
It will stand at the head
of the protest line.
This voice will not be
silenced.
It will not be drowned
like those
of its ancestors.

3

## BABY GIRL

Mum called me *Baby Girl*
for 6 months after I
entered this world.

She couldn't think of a name.

I often feel like a baby girl—

Naive and sensitive
Crying and trying
to take my first
clumsy steps.

In this strange universe.

I lose myself
collecting vomit-green money
that is used to define
me as if I were a word
in a dictionary.

The world becomes exhausting
for a baby girl.

## Awkward Feet

2013 I squeezed large feet
into damp, moldy shoes
thin as paper
clinging to me,
cutting my
calluses.
Punish me you did,
with fat bunions
that would join me on
my journey
from youth to now.
Crooked toes in
silver heels at prom.
Limp in my stride
from a bent heel
to
curved calloused soles
flying down a track
to
tight ballet shoes
to
May 2020 when dainty toes
carry me down
the aisle to my diploma.
I crawled, I stumbled, I fell, I stood.
You picked me up every time.

## Once a month

My uterus is the enemy.

7 days

Pain swallows me whole

Pulsing angrily, it is
unforgiving, merciless
rage ripping me apart.

Imprisoned by my body,
hot and cold,
shivering and sweating,

I can't speak, think, move.

## Hair Trilogy

I.

Wild jungle
won't be tamed.
She bends, stretches her
coils to heavens.

Tangled, matted mess,
I wanted her gone.

She's here to stay.

II.

She started small.

As she grew,
so did my love for her.

Her shrinkage, coarse,
delicate charm,

styled for protection.
Wiry nest of good hair.

4C beauty,

She's here to stay.

III.

Crown on my head.
My fro.

All she wanted was
love,
water,
moisture.

My curls, my kinks,
spring, reach for the sun,

tussle with gravity,
defy beauty standards.

She's *hair* to stay.

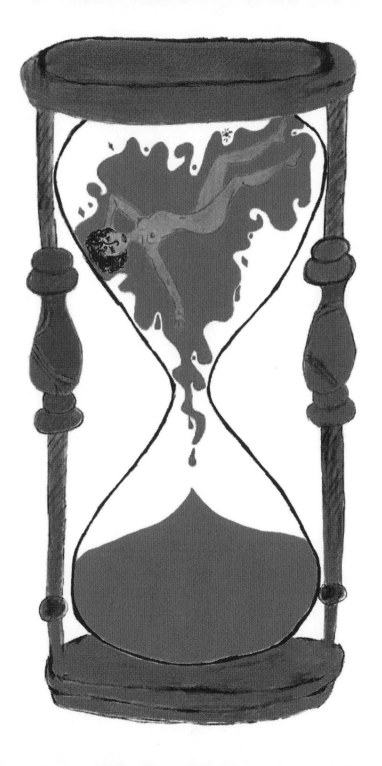

## BLACKOUT

NYC 2003
This city that never sleeps
closed her eyes for 16 hours.
Blackout for all, havoc for most
but on Mexico Street
the universe was merciful...
Four children and their mother sat
around an oakwood table,
with candles foraged from the dusty attic.
Lo mein and broccoli covered sticky fingers.
Their mother's smile was a lantern in the dark,
they all shone,
and their silhouettes
danced in harmony.

## ELEMENTARY GIRLS BALLAD

When we were in elementary school,
I envied your chest.
All the boys liked you;
I too wanted breasts.

I wanted a silky bra.
I yearned to feel grown,
with curves, hips and long hair
that reached my tailbone.

I already had luscious locks,
swinging down my back,
but it seemed like boys didn't
care at all about that.

So I wanted a bra, that pushed
my tiny chest up to my neck,
making everyone stop and stare,
and show me some respect.

I cut elastic stockings, stitched
a makeshift cloth around my midst.
Annoying, sliding fabric.
Why did I even want this?

Along with my period and pimples,
my bosom finally came.
I started wearing bras and
nothing was the same.


Fast forward many years,
I guess I'd say I'm grown.
I mean, it has its perks,
but I wish I would have known:

13

Adulthood comes with bills, stress, and pain.
There's no rush for womanhood.
Strong friendships, love, and freedom arrive
with age, as they should.

I'm in love with my B-cup, my toned legs and arms.
I care about my happiness,
not what men have to say.
My confidence and beauty shine,
so I get them anyway.

I hardly wear bras now.
I prefer to free the nipple.
Funny how times have changed
so much since we were little.

Somewhere in New York, an ice cream truck jingled
Children played double dutch
Crawled over the jungle gym like ants
Eleven year old me
smiled up at the rusted monkey bars.
Even for a tall child they seemed
miles from my grasp.

I wanted to try

to ascend the metal,
climb across, look out,
sit like a Queen on her throne,
and wave a cupped hand.
With quivering legs I crawled to the top;
my pastel blouse turned moist under the armpits.
At the top,
the only thing that met me was fear...
Fear of falling. Fear of hurting.
I was stuck between metal,
legs dangling in mid-air,
looking nothing like a Queen.

Eventually an older boy helped me down.
When my feet landed firmly on the ground,
and air rushed back into my lungs,
I looked up at the bars and I wanted to climb them again.

*-A TIME WHEN I WAS BRAVE*

## OLD FRIEND (HAIKUS)

Dear darling sister,
...Is it hard to remember,
we were ever close?

Or don't you recall
fast hands sneaking ice-cream, and
pinky finger pacts,

wearing matching shirts,
giggling about boys, jumping
rope in the driveway?

Shared no DNA,
yet friendship was woven by
threads of loyalty.

Virgo and Leo.
Earth and fire baby girls,
born a month apart.

Bonded since we crawled;
from bibs and pacifiers
to bras and tampons.

How long has it been
since we walked side by side on
the streets of Brooklyn?

Complicated teens
inspired by tinseltown
ready to leave home.

How many swift years
have passed since sisterhoods' end?
...Regards, Thandiwe.

## MOTHER

With even breath, my heart rate slows.
With eyelids shut, a dream unfolds.
Laughter of a little girl; I'm with you again,
helping you push a glass baking dish in the oven.

The orange of a thousand suns pours through
the window. My nostrils fill with the smell of dew.
Legs dangling from a swing, I shout with glee,
relishing in what you taught me.

Long locks blow in Summer breeze
Jaw unlocked, feeling at ease.
I'm sixteen. Tears stream down my swollen face
*Love hurts* you tell me, and we embrace
How is it that I am made whole;
blessed with a kind, nurturing soul.

Since diaper days, when I was young and naive,
you gave me strength - instilled prosperity.
A mother of four, just like father,
except you didn't leave because you couldn't be bothered.

You persevered and your efforts are shown,
in the now four adults you call your own.
I hope one day I can buy you a home,
a tropical island or a brown stone.

I pondered ways to repay, from dawn until night,
Yet none of my gifts would suffice.
My life would be empty if we didn't have each other,
I'm filled with pride that I can call you my mother.

## FATHER

Not only are you the father of lies,
Easy to despise,
You are also a father of four.
Or five? Have you had more?

Can I ask you something?
Just this once I'd like your attention.
Do you sleep at night undisturbed,
closed eyelids shutting out the world?

Do you drive to work, whenever it is you go,
return at five (let's say) and watch your favorite show?
Has she prepared your favorite dish -
yams, dumplings and ackee with salt fish?

Do you eat then work then sleep?
Receiving cash under the table; the only job you can keep.
Those are only some questions I wish to ask,
I suppose you do complete those tasks.

As you went through life all this time,
have your children ever crossed your mind?
Or do you not care what becomes of us?
If we were left on the streets, swept away in dust.
If we perished from illness and ceased to exist?
Would it trouble your heart to hear of this?

I hardly think of you anymore,
just another black man lost at the store.
Caring for his children became a chore,
so he left them one day with a mother they adore.
One day you'll hear about us and see how successful we've
become,
but it'll be too late, the damage can't be undone.

## Siblings

Even.
Small.
Rolls off the tongue.
A jagged, hollow space
connected by lines and corners.

The number 4.

Beauty comes in fours.

Seasons.
Earth, Air, Fire, Water.
Clubs, Spades, Hearts, Diamonds.

Us.

My brothers and my sister.

How is it that I can look at you from across
an overcrowded room and know what you're thinking?

We are like china dishes
made of bone, and sometimes
chipped at the edges by flaws.
My eldest brother; fearless.
My younger brother; compassionate.
My younger sister; candid.
From baby bottles to diplomas,
a tornado of inside jokes and fist fights;
linked by a fateful friendship.

## A Summer Image

Glistening water
liquid gem
stifling heat.
Mahogany tree
ample branches
stretching its arms
over the heads
of young bodies.
A gift from nature
only a mother could create.
Smiles of joy
on bronze faces,
twirling
stretched
limbs on damp glassy rocks.
The fire in their eyes
The summer's heat
that kisses their skin.

## BARE

I miss being ten years old,
skipping bare backed & breathless
on old nylon carpet, toothy grinned.
Painted with innocence, tickled with curiosity,
ignorant to the meaning of sex,
I was.

It didn't take long for me to catch on;
ingest motion pictures piffle
that forced nudity and sex together
in a country where
nakedness is shameful.

Still,

I've always felt best in my birthday suit,
unadorned and buttered with shea,
sleek with coconut oil, reflecting
ultraviolet radiance.

As I lay on satin, with eyes closed,
I paint trees on bone-white walls,
pretend I'm unclad, embosomed in a garden;
grounded by needled grass root,
sun pressed on my forehead,
charging me like a battery,
living in a place unbound by
society's laws.

## SALTFISH & ACKEE

Saltfish, ackee, fried dumpling, & plantains,
you smell like Christmas mornings
as soca & reggae quaked wooden floors
and mama shook her hips in the kitchen,
arms deep in flour.
Four little ones scrambled at her feet,
waving toy trucks, barbie dolls, and
red wrapping paper,
thinking about how
lucky they were with one gift each.
Sweat shone on round faces
pressed against steamy windows, watching
snow fall outside in frozen air.
Tiny fingers drew
hearts and spirals on foggy glass.
Entertained by
playing cards and
back bending, arms stretching
silly games of Twister.
Mama laughed with stars in her eyes,
hugging her babies,
and we smelled
Saltfish ackee, fried dumpling, & plantains,
the smell of home.

## FRIDAY THE 13TH

Thunder roared and dark skies flashed with lightning rays
On Friday the 13th; a supposedly cursed day.

8 hours of induced labor- of pain
"Make doo-doo," the doctor says again and again

It was shocking that my father was present,
He always missed important events

I was one of 358,891 babies born in the US that day
But others weren't so lucky, I have to say...

"Mother and Baby killed" - The New York Times
As their eyes shut forever, I opened mine
Tupac Shakur; age 25
Today he slipped into eternal sleep
Torture victim sues
Last day for sale on pantyhose: black, brown, nude

I try to find happy articles but I cannot
Only ads, tragic stories, death and whatnot

I awoke on the day of my birth,
to a broken, shattered, Earth.

You are lucky if
You've never forgotten
what zip code was used
for applications.

I've never known permanency.

Only five digit numbers of
locations where I was shaped,
and felt the Earth's teeth.

Family made temporary shelters
home.

We relocated
like chess pieces, and every year,
tax forms made me remember.


*-NOMADS*

## Riches

Silver spoon in mouth
Butler waiting on me
My own room
Fourchu lobster and
other dishes I
couldn't pronounce.
A taste of wealth;
I wanted the lifestyle.

Had I not known broken fans,
a single room with five sleeping bodies,
laying on a kitchen floor listening
to gunshots,

who I would be?

Who would I be?

## La La Land

2,451 miles from home
with my luggage at hand

and nothing but a dream.

To be seen in the
flickering pictures on
flat screens,

I follow a dream.

An unclear path
leads me to
La La Land
with my head
in the clouds

and a dream.

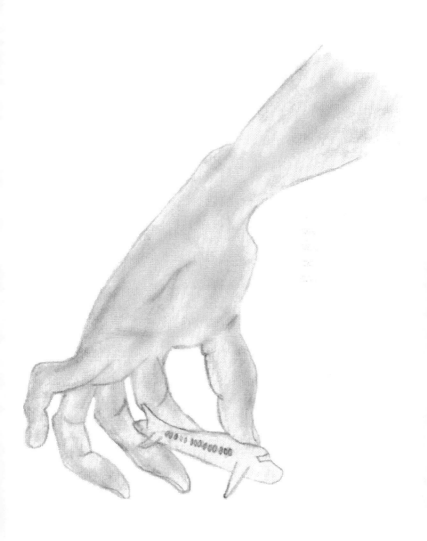

## Leaving Home

Clutter, junk, chaos.
All mine.

Things stacked to the ceiling.

I wanted a life that wouldn't
squeeze me out of my own room.

When did I buy so many things?
Enough to fill a room
Objects I can't take with me after?

In useless pieces of plastic
metal, wood.

Heavy objects weighing me.

I had only intended to bring
what warms my heart,
makes me smile;

Paper letters
written with love,
Smooth bendy photos.

Fragile, light, meaningful.

# Part II:
## Defining Love

## ABOUT LAST NIGHT (BALLAD)

Look at you, sitting here bare chested with drawers on.
Man, you can't stomach what you dish out.
Staring at me with your jaw clenched,
mouth twisted in a pout.

Scowl on your beautiful face.
Believe me, I didn't tell you out of spite,
when I confessed that I stumbled home buzzed,
glassy-eyed, arm linked with another man last night.

You have to understand, I am my own woman.
Flowing like wind. Carefree, young, wild. Single.
Adventure running through blue veins,
and I do like to mingle.

I'm trying not to laugh,
Sorry, my bad.
You ain't my man though,
so why are you mad?

You ran around with every girl on the block.
Remember you and whats-her-name?
Short, blonde, you shared with your homeboys?
So, me and you-know-who - ain't that the same?

Oh stop. You don't need to know who he is.
Just give it a rest.
How about we change the subject?
I think that would be best.

Okay, well if you insist, the Thai wasn't the only
spicy thing he and I had yesterday.
I won't spell it out for you,
but here's what I'll say.

At some point in the future, after I've had my fun,
I will only want one man around.
The day I meet him, I'll let you know,
'cause with you, I don't see myself settling down.

## STRANGER WITH YOUR SCENT (HAIKU)

A man rushed past me.
I inhaled memories and
the bliss of our days.

Carefully crafted, intricate.
Swan white, thin, delicate.
Brimming with possibility,
Written shyly and secretly,
with love, candor,
and a touch of light-hearted banter.
I can imagine him having a think,
sliding his pen across still drying ink.
A faint glow glimmering in day or night
Hunched over a desk, lit by a sliver of light.
Soft print on parchment, now wrinkled with age,
splatters of black on a once blank page.

*-LOVE LETTERS*

## Rare

You are rare
A blue moon on a cloudless night.
If leaving your side meant sipping
sanctified waters from
the fountain of youth
I would choose the path of
crows feet and a shriveled skin suit,
so that I may never leave you.

Tender like mango,
My messy fruit has ripened.
I watch you indulge.

*-BEDROOM STORY (HAIKU)*

The only time falling is ever seen as a good thing
is when it's in love.
*Falling.* The word itself is unstable, dangerous.
So why do I crave the feeling?
The words *I love you* have tumbled from
my lips to few men.
In those moments, if my heart could have spoken, she
would have said
*No, you don't love him.*
*You're in love with the idea of falling.*
*The movie love.*
*The high school love.*
*The grandparents love.*
I knew she was right, but the yearn for love overpowered
me.
It was only when I decided to be in love
with myself first, that I lost the desire to fall.


*-LONGING*

One day I plunged into your world,
accepting your flaws and chipped wings.
A light grew in my dark
Thoughts of a future with you
invaded my mind.
I spun like a top.
Of the billions of people on this planet,
I found one I was in sync with.
I knew I was in love,
and when the words slipped from my lips
like an exhale,
my heart agreed.

*-SOULMATES*

Pinned down, tongue to tongue.
Ardent lover, you fill me in like
a coloring book.

*-BEYOND A KISS*

## The World Knows (Haiku)

Car windows down; soul
exposed, I profess my love,
and the wind listens.

## CLAY GIRL

If you were to take polymer clay
to sculpt your dream girl

She would be
supple and soft russet brown
with a golden heart

She would be me

But
everyone knows
clay hardens with time

I won't be squeezed
between graceless fingers
molded
into yours when

you lack countless traits
you expect from this
dream girl.

## At Last

Pressed against a stone wall,
I held my phone close to the
Spotless window, desperate for wifi.

Trembling.

Was it the wind, or the message on my phone,
signaling Winters' arrival?

*I love you.*

I left you in Brooklyn,
flew to Madrid and started a new life,
Only to read the words I'd longed to hear
when we were together.

Even now,
I don't want to write about you;
you are not worth sharpening a pencil
and pulling out a pad.

Yet here I am.

Standing outside in a dress,
fueled by cheap liquor,

I laugh,

satisfied.

I knew you would love me
long after the final chapter in our book.

Your breath never reeked of guilt.
It was your eyes that betrayed you,

46

both empty and reflecting her image.

You lashed my heart with words,
cutting deeper than any knife.
No surprise there.

Accusation and cruelty
are the songs of the culpable.

You spider of a man, spinning lies,
catching me in your web.
I was a winged creature poisoned by love.
No.
Love is not meant to make one ill.
Let's not call it that.

As I stare at the message on the phone,
Knowing my love for you has drifted off,
never to return,
I taste the sweet perfume of freedom.

## THERE WAS A MAN

There was a man who
crept into my life,
took me by surprise
with his wisdom
and charm.
In his presence,
I tingled
inside from his
golden aura,
that beamed
so bright,
it shone
the path
to my heart.

## Corrupt Love

Is this love?
A burning question
Often leaving me sleepless.
It's what I want to do, you would tell me.
I obeyed, capitulated to your desires.

The word love tainted for eternity.
A girl spellbound from sweet nothings.

It began with my first kiss
Then, can I touch you like this?

You would taunt me for several years,
Just when I thought you'd gone,
you'd reappear.
A never ending game with cards in your hand.
What would be played next?

I'd be taken back to those days,
open-legged I lay.

I wanted boys to like me,
and you said I was pretty.

I was prey and you hunted,
Lured me with flowery words,
Waited for the moment I would be caught in your snare.

And, when I was, the cruelty began.
A dam, barely holding wicked words,
burst open revealing the real you.

*Your breasts are too small*
*You're too skinny.*

A flame of hatred sparked within me.

I was a child still wearing a training bra,
puberty in progress.
My young mind searched for ways to please you,
Wanting your approval

Until I didn't.

How I broke the cuffs of oppression,
sailing away with self-esteem is unknown to me.

How strange that you once seemed so important.
Now you are a nuisance.
An insect buzzing near my head,
I keep swatting. You still return.

A fly on the wall of my life
Watching and waiting for an opening
in my steel armor of confidence and care.
You'll be waiting forever.

Hands gripping.
Fly unzipping.
Mouth open.
Fingers stroking.
Back arched.
Throat parched.
Toes curled.
Hair whirled.
Numb feet.
Damp sheet.
Lights dim.
Naked skin.
Turned on.
Clothes gone.
Windows steamy.
Faces gleamy.
Eye contact.
Muscles contract.
Heart beats fast.
Moments pass.
Love making.
Breathtaking.

-*MIDNIGHT DANCE*

## SAN MIGUEL DE ALLENDE

People loved my chinos
& called me *morena*.
I ate fish tacos and *enmoladas*.
You carried me on your back
Our skin turned bronze under
the festering sun.

Under crescent moon and disco balls
my arms snaked around
your shoulders.
Your hands on my back, strummed
me like a guitar.
Our days were crystal hot springs,
*Milcheladas*,
open car windows on the highway,
sleeping past roosters' morning calls.
Visiting Mexico was planned,
Falling in love, was not.

We ran on cobbled stone
like children at recess.
Midday,
a roasting sun
and the heat of
our passion,
left me dehydrated.

-A Happy Day

# PART III:
# SOMETIMES THE SUN DOESN'T RISE

My body is wind and speed.
I am fire and force on a track,
flying past start like a steed.

Doubts and fears tumble
from my skin with sweat droplets.
If only I could leave my baggage,
my lows, my regrets.

I run for freedom.
I run from old pain,
that on a disk-shaped track
I'm bound to meet it again.

*-FLIGHT*

## SUICIDAL THOUGHTS

Dead leaves have fallen
Snow has melted, and
clocks have gone forward an hour,
since my brain was fogged with
unspeakable thoughts that
ended with my funeral.

An article of clothing I wore in life,
for an interview, a date, a wedding,
will be what I wear for eternity.
If I end up in the Earth sooner
than I should, perhaps it will be the
burgundy shirt mum loves.
Maybe the violet blouse
with the iron stain on the back,
that will go unnoticed
as tear droplets drip onto
a face that is no longer mine.

I will watch from the ceiling,
neither happy nor sad.
Like candle wax,
my body will melt away.
Before the flame expires
into charcoal grey,
my spirit will be with
the ancestors.

It's been years since you died.
The pain is raw. I loathe it.
It sits like a prisoner,
locked behind my chest,
beyond my rib cage.
If time heals all wounds,
this is a life-long sentence.


-GRIEF

## Night Lullaby (Haiku)

A single tear slips
in my ear. I hear faint strums
from songs of sorrow.

Mind blurred by envy
at what you could never be,
and her name was me.

*-HAIKU TO MY LOVER'S MURDERER*

I wish healing was easy.
I wish I could find cures in people.
My wounds are gaping, empty holes.
I make a mess mending them.

-*TRYING*

## THE WORST OF DAYS

Grey clouds and
frost ascending buildings
announce
Winter's presence,
as do the ginger colored leaves crunching
beneath boots.
Withered flowers, dehydrated and crumpled,
laying on concrete, somehow still beautiful.
The Sun is unseen and
violent winds have snaked past my coat sleeve,
up my arm.

I do not shiver.

I have carried Winter with me in
Summer, Spring, and Autumn.
It followed me into my home
and settled under the sheets with me.
It whispered horrors in my ear
whenever I managed to leave the bed.
It held a bottle to my lips once,
as I drank myself into oblivion.

My mind doesn't know how to rid myself of it,
so I wait for a gentle reminder,
that my summer will come again.

## Seeds

Budding seeds
of regret
planted
in the pit of my belly
Sprout
into resentment.
Bulbs aren't happy
without sunlight
and you stole
my light
with your
conditional love
and disapproval.

Years after the funeral,
with pools in your eyes
and shaken breath,
you smiled your broken smile,
you said, *only God could fix.*

*My son never loved any girl but you,*
*what did you do?*

I didn't know.

Now I do.

I was buzzed on life and youth,
a baby bird leaping from a nest,
dancing to the music of the universe.

I was me.

-FOR LOLY

## As I lay me down to sleep

In my dreams, we live a life you were meant to have.
In tranquil oblivion, we travel valleys of my mind.
Time is absolute in slumber.

We float in the vibrant realm of sleep noiselessly,
weightless bodies entwined.
In my dreams, we live a life you were meant to have.

Your hair is soft as wool from Merino sheep.
As you lay on my chest, hand in mine,
Time is absolute in slumber.

Our worlds are in sync; our bond, deep;
I leave all pain behind.
In my dreams, we live a life you were meant to have.

We ride on waves of you and me;
fleeting moments of pleasure, I find.
Time is absolute in slumber,

and death is the sister of sleep.
I'll soon awake and you will only live in my mind.
In my dreams, we live a life you were meant to have.
Time is absolute in slumber.

Sometimes emotion punches me in the stomach
so hard I crumple
to my knees like paper.
I don't understand how, after all these years,
something as simple as ironing a shirt can
stamp your image in my mind.
My eyelids are shut like curtains.
I see your dimple,
your grin,
the freckle on your ear.
I taste your breath.
Your hands reach for mine,
I open my eyes, fingers extended
to pull you in,
and you are gone.

-MEMORIES

## Tangible

If my trauma was
tangible
I would stuff it
into a navy blue suitcase
and toss it into the matching
Ocean, to be consumed
by rogue waves.
The sea would
save me,
take my pain
in her infinite depth;
let me
walk this Earth
without
the aged scars that
eat me alive.

## TO THE MAN WHO PULLED MY SHIRT DOWN

My bare breasts were
two stars
in midnight sky.
They should have been
pictures from the frames
of your
twisted imagination.

My confidence was snatched
with my sleeveless white top.

Cheeks flushing crimson,
my throat closed;
I choked on
a poison called

humiliation.

## BROKEN

I miss you more than you will ever know.
People keep telling me to move on-
you would have wanted me to be happy.
The words *move on* hurt almost as much as the pain of
losing you.
I swallow my hurt.  My eyes burn from hiding a waterfall.
I tell myself not to voice my sadness.
A part of me hates them a little
for adding pain to my pain.

I have lost a lover, and a friend.

I am drenched in sad, but cannot show it
lest a door is shut in my face by those who
don't try to understand.
So i keep it inside until
I am alone.
In my room,
I turn on a fan to muffle the sounds of my
sobs in echoing emptiness.

## Healing

They tell me that to heal I need to
forgive, make peace, move on.

Words tumble
from unknowing lips of people
trying to tell my story.

Blood flows from my
broken flesh
Aura emanates my
fragmented soul.

I want to heal,
find peace,
stitch the wound
that is my destruction.

## Luz

I remember you.
but not your name's spelling, so
I will call you Luz.

Light, in Spanish.

Luz, a dazzling beam in a dark world.
Your parents didn't think so.

Thoughts of you emerge sometimes.

We used to put shirts on our heads,
pretend it was long hair,
play patty cake in the living room.

Sunken cheeks,
toothy smile behind
cinnamon brown hair.
The sound of your
stomach grumbling.
Your stepfather starved you.
Your mother watched.
Your step sister ate.

You ran up dirty steps
of the homeless shelter to
my mother,
where you ate peanut butter and jelly,
played hand games with
my sister and me.
As quickly as you came with your Luz,
your flame was extinguished.
Gone.
Where are you now Luz?

Luz?

Spoon fed self-hate.
Drunk on shame.

My young mind was a vacuum,
ingesting grisly words.

When you are shoved into dirt,
Broken down,
told you are worthless,

you believe the lie.

Then, like a summer breeze
Truth brushed my finger tips, and
I broke free.

*-EMOTIONAL ABUSE*

## DESTRUCTION

Online. Top page. First article:
Instructions on how to kill.
These insects mated, birthed too many
blood red babies
fluttering in abundance,
showing off mother nature's art.

They want us to kill you.
The poisonous words never leave my lips.

My friend says you're supposed to kill them.
She doesn't hesitate. She does so with excitement.

They destroy trees,
which destroys Earth,
which destroys us.

I watch them float,
step over their heaping beauty,
because I know

we are them.

We destroy trees,
which destroys Earth,
which destroys us,
and the powerful kill us.

When using a sewing machine,
fabric is held fast by thin push pins,
fed to a hunk of metal,
where it is stitched into
something pretty.

She hums her
clamorous sound of pleasure
And if you keep feeding her cloth,
she eats it up and fashions
whatever you desire.

My thoughts escape me.
My foot deepens on the pedal.
A pin prick. I remember the favor.

My taut flesh opens like edamame.
Though she is the snake,
I hiss at the sting of betrayal,
and I wonder why I adore her.

She, who does me favors,
as long as she's coddled,
punishes me if I stray.
I am tied to her by an invisible knot
and something called love, so
I always do as she wishes.

*-TOXIC*

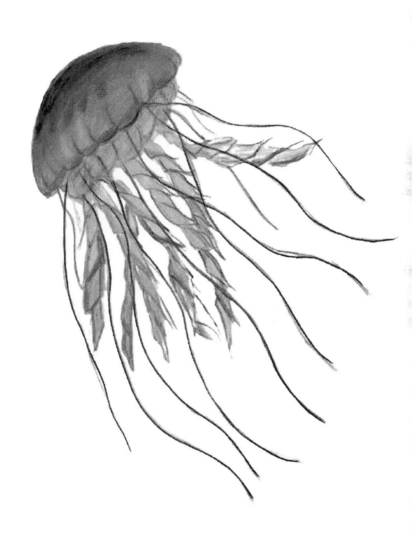

## A Night Out

I know your type;
reeking of misogyny, fake confidence and swagger, crude
and impolite.
You can't take no for an answer.

Vodka on stale breath and hunting with hunger in your
eyes,
my dancing silhouette under disco balls catches your sight.
I know your type.

Forcefully "asking" to dance; pretending to be one of the
"nice guys".
Following girls around the dance floor all night.
You can't take no for an answer.

It's easier for a woman to feign interest and lie.
So, when you asked for the beautiful lady's number, I said
alright.
I know your type.

All next day my phones buzzes with your texts; I finally
reply:
*Thank you, but no thank you*, and you respond with spite.
You can't take no for an answer.

I read your words: *black monkey, whore.* Your hatred
vocalized.
Sick from rejection. Sick from booze.
Sick from pride in your skin being white.
I know your type.

For you, my blackness, intelligence and eloquence, makes
me easy to despise.
If you're going to be a racist, spell Ku Klux Klan right.
You can't take no for an answer.

You. A pig in disguise.
You. Whiny. Entitled. Uptight.
I know your type;
You can't take no for an answer.

I can hear the drums.

*Shhh.*

*Do you hear that?*

*Faint rhythmic banging and buildup.*

*No?*

Why can no one else hear the drums?
Thumping, rising, falling. Rising again.
A loud tap. A bellowing echo.

It must be my heart.
That's the only explanation.
The drums only come sometimes...
When my finger grazes the rusted knob of the old creaking
door to my room after a day out
If I turn a corner on a silent night,
my back erect, my fists balled up
As I jog by a black car with tinted windows,
the engine humming
When I hear a knock from an unexpected visitor.

I hear the drums.

I taste the drums.

Salty flavor of fear and anxiety.
A hand held on my heart.
A sea on my brow.

I hear the drums.

-*STRANGE MUSIC*

# PART IV:
# QUESTIONING CHAOS

## Alternate Universe

If dreams are glimpses of other dimensions,
my other selves are seldom melancholy.

I want their happiness.

In those dimensions they dream as well, wondering the
same thing.

They want my happiness.

## New Normal

While Men fall from sickness en masse
Birds glide- winged beauties above a pier
The Earth is now their own

Every tree, every ocean, every flower, every stone
Power in their stride, change in the air
The Earth will heal herself alas

The Earth will heal herself alas
Creatures rise from grey shadows without fear
The Earth is now their own

Dolphins appear, wild boar roam
Sapphire skies, fresh and clear
The Earth will heal herself alas

Land, sea, sky; the presence is shown
Of ducklings frolicking, elephants singing, aware
The Earth is now their own

Men are weak. Trapped. Alone
Blissful orange, daffodil season, new Spring here
The Earth will heal herself alas

The Earth is now their own

## BEETLE

I watch you crawl.
Ashen shadow on rutted wall.

Unwelcome guest, you are.

I could seal your fate;
smear ivory white with red.
But, who am I?

I am no God,
so
I will let you live.

I let you live. I let you live.

I find you

tangled in a spiders web.

Good deeds done and no good end.

Dandelion,

How do you live
unattached,
hanging to stem by a thread,
sailing in wind indiscriminately,
then letting go, bidding farewell to the other seeds?

If you had a mind, would you ever wonder
how the other seeds were doing?

Would you feel so inclined to
write them; emptying your desires
to meet them again and wait for their response?

Are you like me?
I never want to let people go.
The girl on the bus I sat next to for a few hours.

The lady on the plane who understood when I
told her about my loss.

The man from the hostel.

I find a home in strangers.
I am comforted by people who I should only
pass by and never see again.

I want to take them with me though some live across the
ocean.
I want to know their story and
what they dream about.
Goodbye has never crossed my mind.

Dandelion,

How do you live unattached?

*-Bond*

## APOCALYPSE (HAIKU)

Bare, deserted land.
We could only wonder: 'What's
next?' And the Earth slept.

Of all the words that exist,
how can someone so accurately describe
my life in song and sweet melody,
without even knowing me?
Guitar and piano ring in my ears,
vibrate in my chest;
I feel heard.

-MUSIC

## WAKEUP

Four walls
inside a white picket fence

Job decaying the spirit
Eat. Sleep. Work. Repeat.

Fruitless life.

The days are one.

Until one day,
dipping toes into a pool
of possibility,
you see the world,
unmasked.
Small and vivid as marbles
in the palm of your hand.

Book the flight,
Indulge.
Explore.
Live.

Be Bowie's Major Tom,
Aligned with the universe.

## Pandemic

Feeling like an animal
caged in a 10 by 10 cell with my thoughts
louder than the deafening silence;

The day before

I was free.

Breathing in salty sea air
wind kissing my damp cheeks
sand caressing my glazed skin.

I was free.

Golden day, a dot in time
on this blissful paradise,

I was free.

God is
moon
sun
stars
Earth.

She gives me

eyes and I marvel at nature's canvas
My mouth tastes her bountiful gifts
My feet ground me
I inhale her sweet perfume,
listen to her guidance.

I believe in her,
and She in me.

*-GOD IS THE UNIVERSE*

They stroke the crook of my neck
as you pull me in for a kiss;
undo buttons of my jeans
before we make love.
Scramble eggs in a frying pan,
on Saturday morning.
Take me by the fingertips and twirl me in a circle.

Callused hands, tender on my skin,
covering me with goosebumps.

These hands I love.

They hold your gun as you
sit in a car with your badge glimmering
like a sacred jewel.
You have never pulled the trigger;
I wonder if you ever did-
Would those hands I love ever feel the same?

*-Fears*

Smiling and nodding like
a puppet at
people I'll never know,

lowering my voice
at restaurants,

not dancing
to my music on the bus,
and
How do you do?'s
And I'm good and you?'s
And job?
          Job?
                    Job?
And money?
      Money?
      Money?
And no.
And you shouldn't.
And why be an actress?
And money?

And-

 shut up.

*-SOCIETAL NORMS*

## Black Box

An audience awaits.
Expectant.
In this black box
they go to
forget,
to enjoy.

Anything.

A single spotlight ascends,
like the moon cueing
transformation.
Unzipping,
I hang myself up like
a costume in a wardrobe.

I am someone else for 90 minutes.

Curtains part.
Beady eyes under a cloak of darkness,
follow this person I've become.

They'll discover who she is.

The show has begun.

1/125th of a second.

Some are faster.

Clunky instrument that's said to
steal precious moments
meant to be lived in.

With you, I can relive.

When my loved ones are
mountains and oceans away,
or playing in permanent paradise,
I lean on you.

Memories pop in my head like ads.
I open your digital door, and you

-capturer of moments in time
with effortless clicks-

Give me a present,
I humbly accept:

a photo.

*-CAMERA*

# PART V:
# RAINBOWS AFTER STORMS

I can tell you what I am not,
but I will tell you what I am;

my own.

-REMINDER

I live with freedom, and the breath of
galloping wild horses,
so that one day after I've
blown out hundreds of birthday candles,
witnessed thousands of sunsets,
and turned the world inside out
emptying my bucket list;
standing a foot shorter,
with skin like parchment
and splintery bones,
I can say,

I've lived.

*-FULFILLMENT*

I want to run to the edge of a cliff
and scream ...
Until my tonsils fold
and I bend in half
Until my throat quakes like a frog
and tiny creatures
are no longer frightened
by my thunder
Until despair, worry, and fear
fly out of my spirit
like raging hornets
Until California floats off
until humans move to Mars
Until the Sahara freezes over.
Until....

*-RELEASE*

It can't be
scooped into a measuring cup,

laid flat on a scale,

typed into a calculator,

placed next to a ruler.

Only one person can
measure it;

Me.


*-SELF-WORTH*

Some days when the sun rises, I do not.
I am a wilting flower, expelling dread,
deep in cotton sheets,
stuck in my head.

It's often hard to remember there was a *before*,
and in time there will be an *after*.
Darkness clouding shine will filter with light.
Misery will melt and slip into laughter.

*-LOOKING AHEAD*

They keep insisting that we're enough.
I don't want to be treated like I'm sufficient.
I want to be spoiled like the Earth,
who was only water and land but
wanted more.
Queen of life,
she is rich with color.
Home to glorious beasts,
adorned with flowers.
More than enough.


-*SUFFICIENT*

## I MET AN ANGEL

Are you an angel in disguise?
With ease, I trust you.
Your heavenly home was my safe space.

You calmed the madness in my head.
With your affirming words, I grew.
Are you an angel in disguise?

As I unveiled my story through salted tears,
deep down inside I felt you knew
Your heavenly home was my safe space.

The kindness and love, you spread;
the power and wisdom helped guide me too.
Are you an angel in disguise?

I once walked lonely streets filled with dread,
You saved me from my demons, helped me find a way
through.
Your heavenly home was my safe space.

I can see the radiant future I have ahead,
and I thank you. Still, I must ask you,
are you an angel in disguise?
Your heavenly home was my safe space.

# I GO TO THE BEACH WHEN I NEED TO BE ALONE (HAIKU)

Dandelion dress.
Sandy feet. Salt in my lungs.
Calm in my being.

## FINDING HAPPINESS

I flew across
arid emptiness
mossy woodland
blinding glaciers
frosty tundra
and Atlantic slosh
in search of
something
I could only
find
in the crevices of
my heart:

Joy.

## STORM

The rain hasn't stopped yet,
trees are limp,
tears rolling off their leaves.

The whistling wind warns of a brewing storm.
Damp branches snap.
A daunting silent song manifests.
A magenta purple sky expels fury,
thunder and lightning crack.
Droplets cascade
onto the earthlings below.

Gradually, like a child, the wind is hushed,
ceasing its cry of rage.
Clouds part, unleashing the Universe's fiery star.
A yellow billed cardinal cuckoos, extending wings.
The air smells of sweet soil. The weather is better,
Storms like that don't last forever.

They wore masks here,
long before the pandemic.

Emotion was the disease and
it plagued me.
I didn't understand why, in this place,
sadness was taboo and fake smiles were
the norm.
They didn't know it was okay to not be okay,
And there I was;
a tsunami of emotion and truth,
too powerful to be constrained by an invisible mask.

*-Unguarded*

## Black Woman at a *PWI

Me and my nappy hair and brown skin
on this campus with 6 percent of my black kin.

Tiny liberal arts school; everyone is proud to be left,
yet I still feel like I have the word *target*
on my chest.

*Black lives matter*, they say.

But do they?

All I see is white guilt on white faces.
Where do I fit in, in white spaces?

I'm a little quiet sometimes, so quite frankly,
I'm often mistaken for being angry.

Why shouldn't I be?

I'm at this top-tier college
to get my degree;
nearly straight A student,
still all they can see is

me and my nappy hair and brown skin.

Spouting ugly jokes about affirmative action,
wanting to see the sassy black girl's reaction.
Eager to show they stand in solidarity;
treating black folks like we're some kind of charity,

so I'll spread some clarity.

All we want is equality in the land of the free.

Sick of the same people down with

black folk for the hype,
the first ones to box us into stereotypes.

See, I'm this
multidimensional woman,
I walk around campus with pink
headphones in,
listening to Rihanna and Jay-z,
but I also dig Queen and Vivaldi.

I twerk. I sew. I like making art.
I'm a hopeless romantic.
I can be loud, thoughtful, creative, frantic.

I'm tired of feeling out of place and not being seen.
Most black folks know what I mean.

*Your feelings are valid, we hear you,*
these liberals say.
That's cool, but you *gone* listen today.

## Toxic Masculinity

You are an immense figure
taking up space with
broad shoulders and
coarse hands that
envelop mine.

I cradle you.
You let me into
deep, delicate parts of
your beautiful mind,
that society told you
to hide.

It's girly, they say.

Your rounded shoulders
carry years of
Suppression.

Muted and gazing at open air,
your damp eyes speak
uncertainty,
wondering if I am
judging you.

I see you exposed,
anew,

human.

A shield is meant to protect.
I don't wear it.
I speak of what
hardened me and
prepared my heart for war.

I am exhausted
with the world telling
people to armor up,
swallow their
burning anguish.

I stand ablaze,
Unguarded.


*-VULNERABILITY*

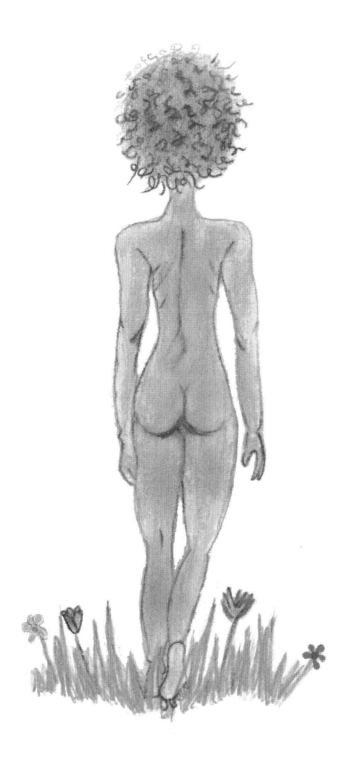

The brow furrows and eyes roll.
Veins thick as slugs on the neck.
A twinge in my belly.
I don't want to give in.
Not so long ago the thought of saying *I'm sorry*
sent tornadoes ripping through my bones.
Fixing a thing I broke is hard
and sometimes I stall.
I've learned it's best to do it quickly.
Like the wings of a butterfly,
some things are fragile; once touched
they may break, never to be repaired again.

*-AMENDS*

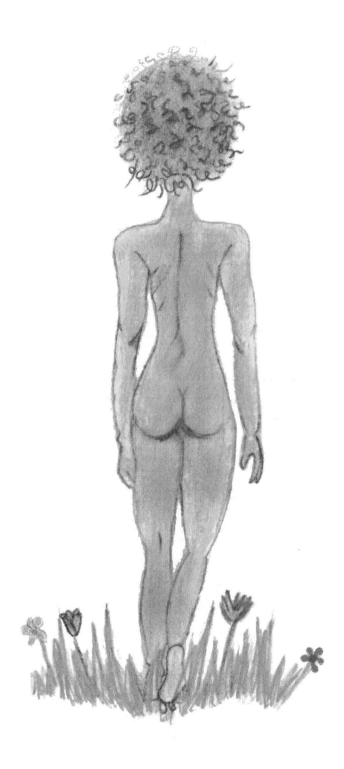

You poured your words into my
head like water.
I rode the waves of your
heart-wrenching story,
and you listened to mine.
For the first time in months,
unjudged and vulnerable,
I felt the cage of my chest open
to release the emotions of a million doves.


*-Exhale*

Dolls with plastic faces,
permanent grins.
Stare too long, they are little devils on shelves.
All smiles. Good vibes.

When the world cries and shakes with fury
they expect good vibes - as if
we are made of plastic.

I will turn to dust before I
lose myself in fake happiness.

Sometimes I open my arms and dance with sorrow.

Everything is not always okay
and that's okay.


*-Toxic Positivity*

## The Wild Unknown

No one can tell her how to feel
or how to deal
With the loss - she is an
insect fighting through thickened moss

And when it occurs
Her known world takes a turn for the worse

For months on end, she is lost.
The journey to happiness, a steepening cost.

Who? What? Where? When? Why?
Why do we have to die?

Who am I? A small speck of flesh in this universe.
At any moment I could be packed into a hearse.

No one knows what to do or say.
To cope, she must create her own pathway.

So she follows the Wild Unknown tarot towards
the suit of wands, cups, pentacles, and swords.

They give her the guidance she needs.
With great enthusiasm she reads.
Every image interpreted by the interpreter.
A spiritual bond glued by the beliefs of the worshipper.

The minor and major arcana
are more useful than a
bunch of people trying to relate.
The cards give answers; they don't hesitate.
Most of all they help her heal.
Those words of wisdom; they make her feel.

The brow furrows and eyes roll.
Veins thick as slugs on the neck.
A twinge in my belly.
I don't want to give in.
Not so long ago the thought of saying *I'm sorry*
sent tornadoes ripping through my bones.
Fixing a thing I broke is hard
and sometimes I stall.
I've learned it's best to do it quickly.
Like the wings of a butterfly,
some things are fragile; once touched
they may break, never to be repaired again.

*-AMENDS*

Not sacred and meant
to strip our power, reduce
us to property.

My body's my own.
Ditching the patriarchy,
leaves them paralyzed.

Well, they don't get to
decide what makes me pure, what
makes me a woman.

*-Virginity (Haikus)*

## POLE DANCER

Mounting stainless steel,
my platform stilettos' immensity
is enough
to cover contorted mouths
spewing foul words.

Stigmatized sport,
you carry me.

A steel woman,
strong woman,
sensual woman,
whose body at 180 degrees
asks, what is gravity?

Superwoman,
bird of paradise,
Jade,
Machine gun,

Names of pole moves.

Shapes of a
confident woman,
brave woman,
dangerous woman.

## Meditation

Instead of watering seeds of sorrow,
I sit cross legged in almost silence,
obediently following breath,
mind never ceasing its murmur.

My own music. I accept it,

leave my body
following the breath.
Hypnotized in a timeless shell.
Here it is inhale, exhale.

I savor this moment like the
last bite of apple pie.

I am seventy-
percent water. They should have
expected my storm.

*-INWARD*

## THE FUTURE (HAIKU)

Rainbows after storms.
A smile on a tired face.
Ready for what comes.

# Mojo

Be still.
Release breath, bubbling inside.
A cauldron.
Time has stopped.
I tumble down like
Alice in Wonderland.
There is no escape but a drink.
Unlike Alice, it won't change my size.

This potion expels a different sort of magic.

Slurred words, stumbling in darkness,
clasping at the air. A curse.
I can count on one hand how many times
I've used alcohol like this.
Three.
Is it the lucky number or the unlucky?
If I tip the barrel, will I return?
Best not to find out.
I do not succumb to poison,
Instead I find another option.

This potion expels a different sort of magic.

A safe space. Coping strategist.
Love.
A gift.
Therapy.

The sun, a lucid light
fueling energy,
bestowing hope.
Winter's black shadow
cast behind.

A tree is with her.
Twisted branches of growth
adorned with silken petals.
New life on an old tree.
Craggy entangle roots
hold stories of the past.
Though some are ugly,
they are needed for growth.

*-JOURNEY*

64560498R00085